singapore
favourites

Delicious recipes from Asia's food capital—including all
the classic Singapore dishes like Chilli Crab, Chicken Satay,
Laksa and Chicken Rice. This fascinating book introduces some
of Singapore's favourite foods, and celebrates the rich and varied
tastes that are the hallmark of Singapore cuisine.

PERIPLUS

Introduction

There can be few places in the world where such a small country can offer such an exciting range of food. Singapore's location at the tip of the Asian mainland made it a natural crossroads throughout history. And when modern Singapore was founded in 1819, the policy of encouraging migrants from nearby Indonesia, as well as from China and India, ensured the mixture of flavours and cooking styles that is the hallmark of Singapore today.

The majority of Singapore's population had its roots in southern China, so southern Chinese regional styles such as Hokkien, Teochew and Cantonese cooking predominate, as well as a number of popular Hakka dishes. The creativity of Chinese cuisine is world renowned. Using a number of basic seasonings (including soy sauce, salted soybeans, ginger, garlic and spring onions) Chinese cooks are able to transform even the most simple foodstuffs into a memorable meal.

The Malays of Singapore, many of whose families came from Java, Sumatra or Malaya, use a wide range of spices and flavourings. Fresh roots such as ginger, turmeric and galangal; fragrant herbs like lemongrass and kaffir lime leaf, and other seasonings including shallots and garlic are partnered with hot chillies to make richly flavoured, curry-like dishes. The soothing creaminess of coconut milk softens many Malay dishes, balancing the heat of the chillies.

Singapore's Indian population originated primarily in the south of the subcontinent, and brought with them a number of styles of cooking, blending a vast array of spices to produce Hindu vegetarian cuisine, lavish Muslim dishes and a wide range of curries, rice dishes and breads.

Living together for close to two centuries, Singaporeans have, to some extent, borrowed each other's cooking styles and ingredients, and a number of distinctively Singaporean dishes have evolved. These might have a Eurasian influence, or perhaps have been created by the Nonyas (Chinese women whose links with Singapore or what was Malaya go back many generations). Others may be an Indian cook's twist on a Chinese noodle dish, or a Chinese chef making the most of fresh chillies.

This fascinating book introduces some of Singapore's favourite foods, dishes that are usually lovingly prepared at home as well as others which are more often enjoyed at the island nation's ubiquitous food courts.

Basic Singapore Ingredients

Bamboo shoots are used fresh, dried or canned in Asian cookery. Fresh shoots are sweeter and crunchier than canned ones. Peel, slice and boil them for about 30 minutes before using. Drain and boil canned bamboo shoots for 5 minutes to refresh them.

Bangkuang is a globe-shaped tuber, tapered slightly at one end like a top, with a papery beige skin covering a crisp, white flesh. Sweet and juicy when small and young, they tend to become fibrous with age.

Belachan is the Malay name for dried shrimp paste. Several types are found, ranging from very moist and black in colour to the light brown, crumbly shrimp paste popular in Malacca. Shrimp paste should be toasted before being used by dry-frying in a pan, placing the *belachan* on the back of a spoon and toasting it above a flame, or wrapping it in foil and grilling it.

Dried black Chinese mushrooms must be soaked in hot water to soften before use, from about 15 minutes to 1 hour, depending on the thickness of the caps.

Candlenuts are waxy, straw-coloured nuts that are ground to add texture and flavour to spice pastes and curry mixtures. Raw cashews or macadamia nuts may be substituted.

Chillies come in many shapes and sizes. The relatively large red or green finger chillies are commonly used in most Singapore dishes. Tiny bird's-eye chillies, also known as *chili padi*, provide more heat. **Dried red chillies** are sometimes preferred for the smoky flavour they give to cooked dishes.

Coconut milk is made by mixing freshly grated coconut flesh with water and squeezing the liquid from the mixture. Add 125 ml ($^1/_2$ cup) water to 3 cups of grated fresh coconut (the flesh from one coconut). Squeeze and strain to obtain **thick coconut milk**. Add 625 ml ($2^1/_2$ cups) water to the grated coconut and squeeze again to obtain **thin coconut milk**. Cans or packets of concentrated coconut milk make a good substitute; dilute according to the instructions for thick or thin coconut milk.

Curry leaves are sold in sprigs of 12–16 small, slightly pointed green leaves. There is no substitute, although they are sometimes sold frozen.

Dried prawns are best kept refrigerated in a humid climate. Look for brightly-coloured, plump prawns. Soak for about 5 minutes to soften.

Hay koh is also known as black prawn paste and is sometimes labelled *petis*. This thick black paste has a strong fishy taste and is used in some Nonya dishes such as Penang Laksa and Rojak sauce.

Kiam Chye (preserved mustard cabbage) is used in some Chinese and Nonya dishes. Soak the heavily salted cabbage in water for 45 minutes to remove some of the saltiness, repeating if neccessary.

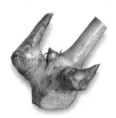

Galangal is an aromatic root used throughout most of Southeast Asia, known as *lengkuas* in Singapore and Malaysia, as *laos* in Indonesia and as *kha* in Thailand. The fresh root can be sliced and deep-frozen for future use.

Garam Masala is made from a blend of spices. It is available premixed from Indian foodstores but is easily made at home. Gently roast 30 g cinnamon sticks, 10 g cardamoms, 5 g cloves, 15 g fennel, 5 g black peppercorns and 4 bay leaves until aromatic then cool and grind to a fine powder. Store in an airtight container.

Ikan bilis, or dried white-bait, are tiny whole fish ranging in size from $1^1/_2$–6 cm ($^1/_2$–$2^1/_2$in). If possible, buy cleaned whitebait which have had the heads and dark intestinal tracts removed; otherwise, snap off the heads and flick out the intestinal tract with the point of a sharp knife for each tiny fish.

Kangkung is a highly nutritious leafy green vegetable also known as water spinach. Young shoots may be eaten raw as part of a salad platter or with a dip. The leaves and tender stems are often braised with chilli and spices.

Lap cheong, or sweet, dried Chinese sausages are perfumed with rose-flavoured wine. They are never eaten alone, but sliced and cooked with rice or other foods.

Noodles are very popular in Singapore and many different types are used. **Fresh yellow egg noodles** (*mee*) are made from egg, wheat flour and water and sold in varying thicknesses. **Rice flour noodles** resemble white spaghetti and are used in *laksa*. **Dried rice vermicelli noodles** or beehoon are thin noodles made from rice flour and water.

Soft tofu

Firm tofu

Pressed tofu
(*Tau kwa*)

Deep fried tofu
(*Tau pok*)

Tofu or bean curd comes in various form. *Soft tofu* is silky and smooth. *Tau kwa* is hard tofu that has been compressed to expel most of the moisture. *Tofu skin* is the dried skin that forms on top of boiling soy milk; it is dried and sold in sheets as a wrapper, or as *tau fu kee*, a thick twisted skin added to meat or vegetable dishes. Small squares of **fermented tofu** are sold in jars. They are either red on the outside, if flavoured with chilli and spices, or creamy white and used as a condiment with rice porridge. Another type of bean curd sometimes added to braised dishes or soups is dried-fried bean curd, *Tau pok,* which is generally sold in small rectangles. These are often sold on strings in Asia, but are elsewhere usually packed in plastic. They are light and spongy in texture, and need to be dipped briefly in boiling water to remove the oil before being used. Dried deep-fried bean curd has as almost nutty flavor and is particularly appreciated for the way it soaks up the liquid to which it is added. It can be kept refrigerated for at least two weeks.

Rice vinegar is a mild and fragrant vinegar. You may substitute distilled white vinegar, however reduce the quantity.

Rice wine is used in many Chinese recipes. The best wine is from Shao Xing in China; substitute sake or dry sherry.

Soy sauce is brewed from soy beans and sometimes wheat fermented with salt. It is salty and used as a table dip and cooking seasoning. The most common type is regular light **soy sauce**, with a medium salty taste. **Black soy sauce** is thicker and less salty with a malty tang. In Indonesia, **sweet soy sauce**, or *kecup manis*, is the most widely used variety.

Star anise is a dried brown flower with 8 woody petals, each with a shiny seed inside, which gives a flavour of cinnamon and aniseed. Use whole and remove from the dish before serving.

Tamarind juice adds a fruity sourness to dishes.

Soak 1 tablespoon tamarind pulp in 60 ml ($^{1}/_{4}$ cup) water, then squeeze and strain the mixture to obtain the juice.

Wild ginger buds, or torch ginger, are the edible bud of the ginger plant. It is sometimes called *bunga siantan* or *bunga kantan* in Singapore.

Yu tiao (Chinese crullers) are 2 long sticks of dough stuck together and then deep-fried. Sometimes called Chinese doughnuts (yu char kway), they are savoury rather than sweet and are traditionally eaten with rice porridge (congee). They are available in Asian fresh markets.

Singapore Rojak
(Spicy Fruit and Vegetable Salad)

$^1/_2$ cucumber, sliced

1 small *bangkuang*, peeled, quartered and cut into thick slices

200 g (7 oz) *kangkung*, cut into lengths and blanched in boiling water for 1 minute

1 square firm tofu or *tau kwa* (pressed tofu), shallow-fried until golden brown, then sliced into 8 pieces

60 g (1$^1/_4$ cups) bean sprouts, blanched for 10 seconds, rinsed and drained

2 slices pineapple, cubed

1 unripe green mango, peeled and sliced

1–2 *yu tiao* (Chinese crullers), cut into 6–8 pieces (optional)

1 wild ginger bud, sliced (optional)

Sauce

2–3 large red finger-length chillies, deseeded and sliced

1 tablespoon shaved *gula melaka* (palm sugar) or brown sugar (page 15)

1 teaspoon *belachan* (dried shrimp paste), toasted (page 3)

2 tablespoons tamarind pulp, soaked in 125 ml ($^1/_2$ cup) water, squeezed and strained to obtain juice

1 tablespoon *hay koh* (black prawn paste)

$^1/_2$ teaspoon salt

75 g ($^1/_2$ cup) raw peanuts, dry-roasted and coarsely crushed in a blender or pounder

1 To make the Sauce, grind the chillies, *gula melaka* and *belachan*, tamarind juice, *hay koh*, and salt to a smooth paste in a blender. Transfer to a bowl, add the peanuts, stir and set aside.

2 Place the rest of the ingredients into a serving dish. Drizzle the Sauce on top and toss to mix. Serve immediately.

Serves 4
Preparation time: **10 mins**
Cooking time: **10 mins**

Popiah (Fresh Spring Rolls)

2 tablespoons crushed chilli flakes or 6–8 red finger-length chillies, deseeded and ground
8 cloves garlic, crushed with a little salt
4 tablespoons *tim cheong* or *kecup manis*
6 large lettuce leaves
1 small cucumber, peeled and finely shredded
100 g (2 cups) beansprouts
1 cake *tau kwa* (pressed tofu) 100 g (3¹/₃ oz), deep-fried until golden, diced
2 hard-boiled eggs, peeled and chopped
2 *lap cheong*, simmered 3 minutes, thinly sliced

Filling
1¹/₂ tablespoons oil
1 small onion, halved, thinly sliced across
2 cloves garlic, minced
4 teaspoons *tau cheo* (salted soy beans—page 19), lightly smashed
100 g (3¹/₃ oz) pork loin, very thinly sliced
100 g (3¹/₃ oz) prawns, peeled, heads removed
250 g (8 oz) boiled or canned bamboo shoot, finely shredded
1 *bangkuang*, (300 g/ 10 oz), finely shredded
1 tablespoon soy sauce
¹/₄ teaspoon ground pepper

Wrappers
125 g (1 cup) plain flour
¹/₂ teaspoon salt
300 ml (1¹/₄ cups) water
5 eggs, lightly beaten
2 teaspoons oil

Serves 4
Preparation time: 50 mins
Cooking time: 50 mins

Tim cheong, or sweet black Chinese sauce, is a fragrant sweet sauce used in many marinades and sauces; substitute *kecup manis*.

1 To make the Wrappers, place the flour, salt and water in a bowl and mix to form a smooth batter. Then add the eggs and mix well. Heat a 20-cm (8-in) skillet, add ¹/₂ teaspoon of the oil to grease the skillet. Add ¹/₂ cup (125 ml) of the batter and swirl the skillet to spread the batter in a thin layer. Cook over moderate heat until the batter sets, about 30 seconds. Flip the batter and cook on the other side for a few seconds. Remove from the skillet, place on a serving plate and cover with a damp cloth. Repeat to make 10 Wrappers.

2 Heat the oil for the Filling in a wok or saucepan. Stir-fry the onion and garlic over low to moderate heat until soft, about 2 minutes. Add the *tau cheo* and stir-fry 1 minute. Increase the heat, add the pork and stir-fry until it changes colour, about 1 minute. Add the prawns and stir-fry 1 minute, then add the bamboo shoots, *bangkuang*, soy sauce and pepper.

3 Stir the mixture and bring to a boil. Then reduce the heat, cover and simmer for 30 minutes, until cooked through. Add 1 tablespoon of water if needed. Transfer the cooked mixture to a bowl and allow to cool.

4 To serve, transfer the Filling and Wrappers to the dining table. Place the chilli, garlic and sweet black sauce in small sauce bowls on the table. Arrange the lettuce leaves, cucumber, bean sprouts, *tau kwa*, boiled eggs and *lap cheong* on a large plate.

5 Smear one side of a Wrapper with chilli sauce, garlic paste and sweet black sauce. Add half a lettuce leaf, some of the Filling, cucumber, bean sprouts, *tau kwa*, egg and *lap cheong*. Tuck in the sides of the Wrapper and roll it up. The Popiah can be sliced into 3–4 pieces if preferred. Repeat to make the rest of the Popiah.

Crispy Fried Ikan Bilis and Peanuts

5 tablespoons oil
150 g (2 cups) cleaned and dried *ikan bilis*
75 g (¹/₂ cup) raw peanuts
6 shallots, diced
1 tablespoon sugar
¹/₂–1 teaspoon chilli powder
¹/₄ teaspoon turmeric powder
1–2 small round limes, halved (optional)

Serves 4–6
Preparation time: **15 mins**
Cooking time: **10 mins**

1 Heat 3 tablespoons of the oil in a wok. Add the *ikan bilis* and stir-fry over medium heat until crispy and golden brown. Remove from the wok and drain on paper towels. Discard the oil and wipe the wok.
2 Reheat the wok over low to medium heat and dry-fry the peanuts until browned, about 8 minutes. Remove from the wok and set aside.
2 Heat the remaining oil in the wok over low heat and stir-fry the shallots for 2 minutes, then add the sugar, chilli powder and turmeric, and cook until fragrant, about 2 minutes.
3 Return the *ikan bilis* and peanuts to the wok and mix thoroughly. Transfer to a plate and allow to cool. Squeeze a little lime juice over the dish just before serving.

Bak Kut Teh (Pork Bone Soup with Spices)

600 g (1¹/₃ lbs) meaty
  pork ribs, cut into pieces
3 cloves garlic, left whole,
  lightly bruised
1 cinnamon stick
2 cloves
1 star anise pod
¹/₂ teaspoon black
  peppercorns
2 teaspoons salt
1 tablespoon black
  soy sauce
1¹/₂ litres (6 cups) water

Sauce
60 ml (¹/₄ cup) black
  soy sauce
1 red finger-length chilli,
  deseeded and sliced

1 Place all ingredients (except the Sauce ingredients) in a heatproof dish with a fitting lid. Place the dish on top of a small plate set in the bottom of a large pot or wok, and add boiling water until it comes half-way up the sides of the dish.

2 Cover the wok or pot and bring the water back to a boil. Then reduce the heat and simmer on low heat until the pork is very tender and almost falling off the bone, about 2¹/₂ to 3 hours. Add more boiling water to the pot or wok as needed.

3 To make the Sauce, pour the soy sauce into 4 small sauce bowls and add sliced chilli to each.

4 Portion the pork bones and stock into 4 bowls and serve with the Sauce on the side.

Serves 4
Preparation time: **10 mins**
Cooking time: **2¹/₂–3 hours**

Salted Vegetable and Duck Soup

This delicious soup tastes even better if kept overnight and eaten the next day. Substitute duck with pork ribs or chicken if preferred. *Kiam chye* is preserved mustard cabbage, and there are two types in the market. One is from China and is sold as pickled pieces in large ceramic jars. It is very salty and needs to be soaked in water for 45 minutes to 1 hour to reduce the saltiness. The other variety is from Thailand and is less salty and has a more sour taste. It is sold in vacuum-packed plastic containers with its juices and is readily available in most supermarkets.

$1/2$ duck (about 1 kg/ $2^1/_4$ lbs)
3 litres (12 cups) water
350 g (12 oz) *kiam chye* soaked in water for 45–60 minutes, then sliced into thick pieces
$1/2$ teaspoon tamarind pulp mashed with 1 tablespoon warm water, strained to obtain juice
3 small tomatoes, about 200 g (7 oz)
1 cm ($1/_4$ in) ginger, peeled and crushed

Chilli Dip
60 ml ($1/_4$ cup) black soy sauce
1–2 red finger-length chillies, deseeded and sliced

1 Quarter the duck with a heavy cleaver, rinse and set aside. Bring $1^1/_2$ litres (6 cups) of water to a boil in a large pot over high heat. Scald the duck in the boiling water for 2 minutes to get rid of the wax and fat. Drain and discard the water.

2 Bring another $1^1/_2$ litres (6 cups) of water to a boil in the pot over high heat. Add the duck, *kiam chye* and tamarind juice and boil for 30 minutes.

3 Add the tomatoes, reduce heat to medium and simmer for 30 minutes.

4 To make the Chilli Dip, pour the soy sauce into 4 small sauce dishes and add some sliced chilli to each.

5 Ladle the *kiam chye*, duck and some soup into individual serving bowls. Serve hot with rice and small bowls of the Chilli Dip on the side.

The Thai variety of *kiam chye* does not need to be soaked in water. Add the juice in the packet with the tomatoes in step 3. If preferred, add salt to taste.

Serves 4
Preparation time: **20 mins**
Cooking time: **1 hour**

Deep-fried Tofu with Peanut Sauce

2 cakes (400 g/14 oz)
 tau kwa (pressed tofu)
Oil, for deep-frying
1 small cucumber
2 teaspoons salt
160 g (2 cups) bean
 sprouts, washed, shells
 and tails removed

Peanut Sauce
4 shallots or $1/2$ red
 onion, peeled
2–3 red finger-length
 chillies, deseeded, or
 2–3 teaspoons crushed
 chilli flakes
2 tablespoons shaved
 gula melaka (palm
 sugar) or brown sugar
 (see note)
80 g ($1/3$ cup) chunky
 peanut butter
4 teaspoons black
 soy sauce
1 tablespoon tamarind
 juice (page 5)
$1/4$ teaspoon salt
60 ml ($1/4$ cup) water

1 To prepare the Peanut Sauce, grind the shallots or onion, chillies and *gula melaka* in a mortar or blender until fine, adding a little water if necessary to keep the mixture turning. Transfer to a bowl, add the peanut butter, soy sauce, tamarind juice and salt, and mix well. Then add the water and mix to make a thick sauce. Set aside.

2 Slice the *tau kwa* cakes into quarters and pat dry with paper towels. Set aside. Heat the oil in a wok until very hot and deep-fry the *tau kwa* until golden brown and crisp, about 4 minutes. Drain on paper towels and allow to cool. Then cut into thin slices.

3 Rake the skin of the cucumber with a fork. Rub the salt into the skin, pushing it into the grooves. Then rinse under running water. Place the cucumber in a piece of cloth and squeeze out as much liquid as possible. Then slice thinly and arrange on a serving dish.

4 Place the tofu slices over the cucumber, and scatter the bean sprouts over them. Drizzle the Peanut Sauce on top and serve immediately.

Gula melaka, or palm sugar, ranges in colour from golden brown to dark brown. It is less sweet than white sugar, and has a maple-syrup flavour. Dark brown sugar or maple sugar make good substitutes.

Serves 4
Preparation time: **15 mins**
Cooking time: **10 mins**

Stir-fried Bean Sprouts with Salted Fish

3 tablespoons oil
4 tablespoons (50 g)
  thinly sliced salted fish
1 clove garlic, diced
250 g (8 oz) bean
  sprouts, rinsed
1 spring onion, cut into
  lengths
Generous sprinkling of
  white pepper

Serves 4
Preparation time: 5 mins
Cooking time: 4 mins

1 Heat the oil in a wok over medium heat and stir-fry the salted fish until golden brown and crisp, about 5 minutes. Remove from the oil and drain on paper towels.
2 Reheat the oil until smoking hot and stir-fry the garlic for a few seconds, then add the bean sprouts and stir-fry over very high heat for 30 seconds. Add the fried salted fish and spring onion, and stir-fry for another 30 seconds; the bean sprouts should be just wilted but not soggy. Do not over cook!
3 Transfer to a serving dish, sprinkle white pepper over the dish and serve with steamed rice.

Malay-style Sambal Prawns

3 tablespoons oil
600 g (1¹/₃ lbs) fresh
  medium prawns
1 tablespoon tamarind
  juice (page 5)
1 onion, thinly sliced
1 tomato, cut into wedges
1 teaspoon salt
1 teaspoon sugar
Coriander leaves, to gar-
  nish

Seasoning Paste
12–15 dried red chillies,
10 shallots, peeled
3 cloves garlic, peeled
2 slices fresh ginger
¹/₂ teaspoon *belachan*
  (dried shrimp paste)

1 Peel and devein the prawns. Rinse and set aside.

2 To make the Seasoning Paste, slice the chillies into short lengths, then soak in hot water for about 10 minutes to soften. Discard the seeds. Grind the chillies and the rest of the ingredients to a smooth paste in a mortar or blender, adding a little oil if necessary to keep the mixture turning.

2 Heat the oil in a wok over medium heat and stir-fry the Seasoning Paste until fragrant, about 5 minutes. Add the prawns and stir-fry until they change colour, about 2 minutes. Add the tamarind juice, onion, tomato, salt and sugar, and gently stir-fry until the prawns are cooked, about 2 minutes.

3 Transfer to a serving dish, garnish with coriander leaves and serve with steamed rice.

Serves 4
Preparation time: **15 mins**
Cooking time: **10 mins**

Singapore Chilli Crab

2 kg (4$^1/_2$ lbs) live mud crabs (2 large crabs)
2 tablespoons oil
6 shallots, diced
6–8 large cloves garlic, minced
3 tablespoons minced fresh ginger
1–2 bird's-eye chillies or 1 red finger-length chilli, deseeded and sliced
875 ml (3$^1/_2$ cups) chicken stock
4 tablespoons hot bean paste or *tau cheo* (salted soybean paste—see note)
4 tablespoons sweet bottled chilli sauce
125 ml ($^1/_2$ cup) tomato ketchup
1 tablespoon sugar
2 tablespoons rice wine
2 teaspoons salt
1 teaspoon white pepper
2 tablespoons corn-starch mixed with 3 tablespoons water
2 eggs, lightly beaten
2 sprigs coriander leaves (cilantro)
2 stalks spring onions
1 loaf of French bread

Chilli Ginger Sauce

6 large red finger-length chillies, deseeded
5–6 cloves garlic, peeled
2 cm ($^3/_4$ in) fresh ginger, peeled
2 teaspoons sugar
$^1/_2$ teaspoon salt
1 teaspoon rice vinegar
1 tablespoon water

1 Put the crabs in the freezer for 15 to 20 minutes to immobilise them. Halve lengthwise with a heavy cleaver, then remove the back and spongy grey matter. Pull the claws free and smash in several places with a cleaver. Cut each half of the body into 2 to 3 pieces, keeping the legs attached.

2 To make the Chilli Ginger Sauce, blend all the ingredients in a mortar or blender. Set aside.

3 Heat the oil in a wok over medium heat and stir-fry the shallots, garlic, ginger and chillies until fragrant, about 3 minutes. Add the Chilli Ginger Sauce, chicken stock, bean paste, chilli sauce, tomato sauce, sugar, rice wine, salt and pepper, and bring to a boil. Then reduce the heat and simmer, for 2 minutes. Add the crabs and simmer uncovered, tossing several times until cooked, about 10 minutes.

4 Add the corn-starch mixture to the sauce and stir until it thickens. Add the eggs and stir gently until they set, then transfer to a serving dish. Garnish with coriander leaves and spring onions, and serve with slices of French bread on the side.

Tau cheo, or salted fermented soybean paste is a seasoning like Japanese miso. The beans are sold in jars and they vary from dark brown to light golden in colour, and are sometimes labelled "yellow bean sauce". The basic salted soybean paste contains only soybeans, water and salt; it is possible also to buy slightly sweetened versions, or those with added chilli. The beans are usually mashed before being used. **Hot bean paste** is made from salted soy beans *(tau cheo)* with added chilli.

Serves 4–6
Preparation time: **60 mins**
Cooking time: **20 mins**

Teochew Oyster Omelette (Orr Chien)

4 tablespoons oil
3 cloves garlic, minced
4 eggs
1 cup raw shucked
  oysters, drained
75 g (1$^1/_2$ cups) bean
  sprouts, rinsed
4 tablespoons soy sauce
1 spring onion, chopped
2 sprigs coriander leaves
  (cilantro), chopped
Pinch of white pepper

Dipping Sauce
3 tablespoons bottled
  chilli-garlic sauce
1$^1/_2$ tablespoons rice
  vinegar
$^3/_4$ teaspoon sugar
1 teaspoon soy sauce

Batter
80 g ($^1/_2$ cup) tapioca or
  rice flour
3 tablespoons plain flour
$^1/_2$ teaspoon salt
250 ml (1 cup) water

1 To prepare the Dipping Sauce, combine all ingredients until the sugar dissolves. Pour into 4 small bowls and set aside.

2 To make the Batter, place both types of flour and the salt into a bowl, gradually add the water and mix to make a very thin batter.

3 Heat 1 tablespoon of the oil in a skillet until very hot. Then add $^1/_4$ of the garlic and stir-fry for a few seconds. Pour $^1/_4$ of the Batter onto the skillet and quickly swirl it so that the Batter forms a lacy pancake.

4 When it starts to set, break an egg over the Batter, spread with a spatula and allow to cook until the omelette is browned. Flip the omelette over and scatter $^1/_4$ of the oysters, $^1/_4$ of the bean sprouts, 1 tablespoon soy sauce, 2 teaspoons each of spring onion, coriander and a dash of pepper. Cook for a few seconds, then fold the omelette in half.

5 Transfer the omelette to a plate and keep warm. Prepare 3 more omelettes in the same way. Serve hot with the Dipping Sauce.

Tapioca flour and rice flour are sold in packets in supermarkets and provision shops.

Serves 4
Preparation time: **10 mins**
Cooking time: **15 mins**

Teochew-style Steamed Fish

1 kg (2 lbs) whole pom-
  fret or other fish, cleaned
1/2 teaspoon salt
1/2 teaspoon sugar
1 tablespoon soy sauce
2 teaspoons rice wine
4 cm (1 1/2 in) fresh
  ginger, peeled and sliced
2 dried black Chinese
  mushrooms, soaked in
  hot water to soften,
  stems discarded, caps
  sliced thinly
2 spring onions, cut into
  short lengths

2 teaspoons oil
1 teaspoon sesame oil
2 sour plums (*sin mui*)
  or 1/3 cup thinly-sliced
  kiam chye (pickled
  mustard cabbages-
  page 12)
Pinch of white pepper
Fresh coriander leaves
  (cilantro), to garnish

Serves 4
Preparation time: 10 mins
  + marinating time
Cooking time: 15–25 mins

1 Make diagonal slits on both sides of the fish. Place the fish on a plate and rub the salt and sugar on both sides of the fish. Drizzle the soy sauce and rice wine over the fish and set aside to marinate for 15 minutes.

2 Scatter half the ginger, mushrooms and spring onions on a plate, then place the fish and the marinade over it. Scatter the remaining ginger, mushrooms and spring onions over the fish and drizzle the oil and sesame oil over it. Place the sour plums or *kiam chye* on the fish and put the plate on a steaming rack inside a wok or steamer, half-filled with boiling water.

3 Cover the wok and steam the fish over high heat until cooked, about 15 to 20 minutes depending on the thickness of the fish. Add more boiling water as needed. The flesh should be white to the bone when fully cooked. Season with pepper and garnish with coriander leaves. Serve hot.

Fried Fish with Spicy Sweet Sour Sauce

Oil, for deep-frying
600 g ($^1/_4$ lbs) white fish
  fillets, cut into thick slices
1 teaspoon salt
$^1/_4$ teaspoon white
  pepper
1 egg, lightly beaten
30 g ($^1/_4$ cup) plain flour
Fresh coriander leaves
  (cilantro) and lettuce
  leaves, to garnish

Sweet Sour Sauce
2 red finger-length chillies,
  deseeded and sliced
4 cloves garlic, minced
1 cm ($^1/_2$ in) fresh
  ginger, minced
2 tablespoons oil
One 350-g (12-oz) can
  diced tomatoes
125 ml ($^1/_2$ cup) water
2 tablespoons bottled
  tomato ketchup
2 tablespoons vinegar or
  lemon juice
2 tablespoons soy sauce
1 tablespoon sugar
1 teaspoon salt
1 tablespoon corn-starch
1 tablespoon water

1 To prepare the Sweet Sour Sauce, process the chillies, garlic and ginger to a smooth paste in a mortar or blender adding a little oil if necessary to keep the mixture turning. Heat the oil in a saucepan and add the chilli paste. Stir-fry over low-medium heat until fragrant, about 4 minutes.

2 Add the diced tomatoes and cook, stirring several times, until they are reduced to a pulp, 5-6 minutes. Add the water, tomato ketchup, vinegar or lemon juice, soy sauce, sugar and salt. Bring to a boil, stirring, and simmer for 2 minutes.

3 Combine the corn-starch and water in a small bowl, then add to the sauce and cook, stirring, until the sauce thickens, about 30 seconds. Keep sauce warm over very low heat while the cooking the fish.

4 Heat the oil for deep-drying in a wok. Pat dry the fish fillets then sprinkle on both sides with salt and pepper. Dip into the egg and then into the flour, making sure the fillets are completely covered. Shake to remove any excess flour, then gently drop the fish into the hot oil and deep-fry until cooked through and golden brown, 3–4 minutes. Remove and place on a serving dish and pour the Sweet Sour Sauce over the fish just before serving. Serve on a bed of lettuce leaves and garnish with coriander leaves.

Serves 4
Preparation time: **20 mins**
Cooking time: **25 mins**

Classic Fish Head Curry

1 large fish head, (1$^1/_2$ kg/3$^1/_2$ lbs) cleaned
4 teaspoons salt
4 tablespoons oil
1 teaspoon brown mustard seeds
3–4 sprigs curry leaves
4 cups (1 litre) thin coconut milk
125 ml ($^1/_2$ cup) tamarind juice (page 5)
1$^1/_2$ tablespoons sugar
2 medium onions, peeled and quartered
3 medium tomatoes, sliced in wedges
8–10 small okra

Chilli Paste
15–20 dried red chillies, cut into short lengths and soaked in hot water
8–10 shallots, peeled
3 cloves garlic, peeled
4 cm (1$^1/_2$ in) fresh ginger, peeled and sliced

Spice Mixture
2 tablespoons coriander powder
1 tablespoon cumin powder
1 tablespoon fennel powder
1 teaspoon white peppercorns
1 teaspoon turmeric powder
$^1/_2$ teaspoon fenugreek seeds, ground

1 Thoroughly wash the fish head, remove any scales and season on both sides with 2 teaspoons of the salt, then set aside in the refrigerator while preparing the other ingredients.

2 Grind all the Chilli Paste ingredients to a smooth paste in a mortar or blender, adding a little oil if necessary to keep the mixture turning. Set aside.

3 Combine the Spice Mixture ingredients and set aside.

4 Heat the oil in a large pot or wok and stir-fry the mustard seeds and curry leaves until the seeds start to pop. Add the Chilli Paste and stir-fry over medium to low heat until fragrant, about 4 minutes. Add the Spice Mixture and stir-fry for 2 minutes. Pour in the coconut milk, stirring to mix with the paste and spices. Add the tamarind juice, sugar, onions and the rest of the salt. Bring to a boil, stirring constantly, then reduce the heat to medium and simmer, uncovered, for 5 minutes.

5 Rinse the fish head thoroughly under cold running water. Add the fish head, tomatoes and okra to the pan and simmer, uncovered, until the fish is tender, about 10 to 15 minutes. Serve with steamed rice.

Serves 4–6
Preparation time: **20 mins**
Cooking time: **20 mins**

Indian Mee Goreng (Indian-style Fried Noodles)

500 g (1 lb) *mee* (fresh
yellow noodles)
$^1/_4$ cup (60 ml) oil
100 g ($3^1/_3$ oz) *tau kwa*
(pressed tofu), diced
12 curry leaves, minced
(optional)
1 medium onion, diced
1 ripe tomato, diced
1 tablespoon bottled
sweet chilli sauce
3 tablespoons bottled
tomato ketchup
1 tablespoon soy sauce
2 eggs, lightly beaten
1 potato, boiled, peeled
and diced
1 spring onion,
sliced (optional)
1 finger-length chilli, sliced
1 cucumber, sliced
(optional)

1 Place the noodles in a colander and rinse well under running water. Drain thoroughly and set aside.

2 Heat the oil in a wok over high heat and stir-fry the *tau kwa* until golden brown, about 3 minutes. Remove from the oil and drain on paper towels.

3 Add the curry leaves, if using, and onion to the wok and stir-fry over medium heat until soft, about 4 minutes. Add the drained noodles, tomato, chilli sauce, tomato ketchup and soy sauce, and stir-fry for 3 minutes.

4 Add the beaten egg and allow to set, then mix well with all the ingredients in the wok. Add the potato and *tau kwa*, and stir-fry just enough to heat through, about 1 minute. Add the spring onion, and mix well. Transfer to a large serving dish and scatter the sliced chillies on top. Serve hot with small sauce bowls of tomato and chilli sauce, and freshly sliced cucumber on the side.

Serves 4–6
Preparation time: **10 mins**
Cooking time: **15 mins**

Mee Siam (Rice Vermicelli in Sweet Thai Gravy)

1 litre (4 cups) water

3 tablespoons dried prawns, soaked to soften, drained and blended to a powder

2 tablespoons tamarind pulp soaked in 125 ml ($^1/_2$ cup) water, mashed and strained to obtain juice

100 g (2 cups) bean sprouts

1 spring onion, sliced into short lengths

300 g (10 oz) cooked prawns (see note)

300 g (10 oz) *beehoon* (dried rice vermicelli), soaked in hot water to soften, drained, then torn into lengths

1 cake (100 g/$3^1/_3$ oz) *tau kwa* (pressed tofu), deep-fried until golden, then thinly sliced

2 hard-boiled eggs, peeled and quartered

2 limes, quartered

Spice Paste

8–10 dried chillies, cut into short lengths, soaked to soften, then deseeded

8 shallots, peeled

6 candlenuts, roughly chopped

4 tablespoons oil

$^1/_4$ cup *tau cheo* (salted soy beans—page 19), crushed with the back of a spoon

1 tablespoon sugar

1 To prepare the Spice Paste, grind the chillies, shallots and candlenuts in a mortar or blender, adding a little oil if needed to keep the mixture turning.

2 Heat the oil in a wok over medium heat and stir-fry the Spice Paste until fragrant, about 4 minutes. Add the *tau cheo* and stir-fry for 30 seconds, then sprinkle in the sugar and stir-fry for another 30 seconds. Remove from the wok and place the mixture in a small bowl.

3 Place half the Spice Paste in a large saucepan. Add the water and ground dried prawns, and bring to a boil. Then add the tamarind juice, reduce the heat to medium and simmer for 3 minutes. Remove from the heat and set aside in a warm place.

4 Return the remaining Spice Paste to the wok, add the bean sprouts and stir-fry over high heat for 30 seconds. Add half the spring onions and prawn, and stir-fry for 30 seconds. Add the *beehoon*, a little at a time, stirring briskly to mix well, about 2 minutes.

5 Serve the noodles in individual bowls as shown, topped with spring onions and prawns and garnished with *tau kwa*, eggs and lime. Pour the gravy over the noodles at the table.

To prepare the prawns, cook fresh prawns in a pot of boiling water until the prawns turn pink, about 3 to 4 minutes. Then drain the prawns in a colander and set aside to cool. Peel the prawns, discard the heads, gently devein then halve each prawn lengthwise.

Serves 4–6
Preparation time: **45 mins**
Cooking time: **30 mins**

Singapore-style Laksa
(Noodles with Coconut Gravy)

500 g (1 lb) fresh round laksa noodles, blanched for 30 seconds
100 g (2 cups) beansprouts

Coconut Gravy
10–12 dried chillies, cut into lengths, soaked to soften, deseeded
2–3 red finger-length chillies, deseeded and sliced
16 shallots, peeled
6 cloves garlic, peeled
5 cm (2 in) fresh galangal root, peeled and sliced
2 cm (3/4 in) fresh ginger, peeled and sliced
2 cm (3/4 in) fresh turmeric root, peeled and sliced

1 1/2 teaspoons *belachan* (dried shrimp paste), toasted (page 3)
3 stalks lemongrass, thick bottom third only, outer layers discarded, inner part thinly sliced
4 tablespoons oil
2 teaspoons coriander powder
50 g (1/2 cup) ground dried prawns
750 ml (3 cups) water
4 sprigs *daun kesum* (laksa leaves)
1 1/2 teaspoons salt
1 1/2 teaspoons sugar
750 ml (3 cups) thick coconut milk

Garnishes
400 g (14 oz) cooked prawns, peeled
12 fishballs, boiled for 5 minutes, then sliced (optional)
12 hard-boiled quail eggs, peeled (optional)
4 large pieces *tau pok* (deep-fried tofu), blanched in boiling water for 30 seconds, then sliced
4 tablespoons minced *daun kesum* (laksa leaves)

Serves 4–6
Preparation time: **40 mins**
Cooking time: **25 mins**

1 To make the Coconut Gravy, grind the chillies, shallots, garlic, galangal, ginger, turmeric, *belachan* and lemongrass to a smooth paste in a blender, adding a little water if necessary to keep the mixture turning.

2 Heat the oil in a large saucepan, add the chilli paste and stir-fry over medium heat until fragrant 5 to 10 minutes. Add the ground coriander and stir-fry for 1 minute. Add the dried prawns and stir-fry for 1 minute. Add the water, *daun kesum*, salt and sugar and bring to a boil. Reduce the heat to medium and simmer, uncovered, for 5 minutes. Add the coconut milk and bring almost to a boil, then quickly remove from the heat. Discard the *daun kesum*.

3 To serve, divide the noodles and bean sprouts into 4 large serving bowls. Fill each bowl with the Coconut Gravy and top with the prawns, fishballs, quail eggs, if using, and *tau pok* slices. Garnish with laksa leaves and serve immediately with small bowls of chilli or Sambal Belachan (page 35) and lime wedges on the side.

If fresh laksa noodles are unavailable, use 250 g (8 oz) dried laksa noodles, prepared according to directions on the pack, or 200 g (7 oz) *beehoon* (dried rice vermicelli), soaked to soften, immersed in boiling water until soft, then drained.
Daun kesum or *daun laksa* is the local name for the pungent, long-leafed herb also known as Vietnamese mint or polygonum.

Singapore Hokkien Mee
(Mixed Braised Noodles)

250 g (9 oz) dried thick egg noodles or 450 g (1 lb) *mee* (fresh yellow noodles)

150 g (5 oz) *beehoon* (dried rice vermicelli), soaked in hot water to soften, drained and cut into lengths

500 ml (2 cups) water

250 g (8 oz) pork fillet

3 tablespoons oil

300 g (10 oz) small fresh prawns, peeled and deveined, heads and shells reserved

8–10 cloves garlic, smashed

2 eggs, lightly beaten

150 g (3 cups) bean sprouts, rinsed

1 teaspoon salt

$1/2$ teaspoon ground white pepper

1 spring onion, cut into short lengths

4 small limes, halved, to garnish

Sambal Belachan

4–6 red finger-length chillies, deseeded and sliced

$1/4$ teaspoon salt

1 teaspoon *belachan* (dried shrimp paste), toasted (page 3)

Serves 4–6
Preparation time: **25 mins**
Cooking time: **25 mins**

1 To make the Sambal Belachan, grind the chillies, salt and *belachan* finely in a mortar.

2 If using dried noodles, soak the noodles in boiling water for 1 minute, then drain and add to the bowl with the *beehoon*.

3 Bring the water to a boil in a small pot. Add the pork and cook over high heat for 10 minutes. Then drain and set aside to cool, reserving the stock. When cooled, slice the pork into thin strips and set aside.

4 Heat 1 tablespoon of the oil in a saucepan over medium high heat and stir-fry the reserved prawn heads and shells until pink, about 2 minutes. Add 250 ml (1 cup) of the pork stock and bring to a boil. Reduce the heat to medium and simmer, covered, for 5 minutes. Then strain the stock and discard the prawn heads and shells. Return the stock to the pan, add the prawns and simmer until just cooked, about 3 minutes. Strain and reserve the stock and prawns separately. (The recipe can be prepared in advance to this stage and kept refrigerated for several hours.)

5 Heat the remaining 2 tablespoons of oil in a wok over medium heat and stir-fry the garlic until golden brown, about 2 minutes. Discard the garlic. Increase the heat to high and when the oil is very hot, add the eggs and stir-fry for 1 minute. Add both types of noodles, the bean sprouts and 125 ml ($1/2$ cup) of the reserved stock, and stir-fry for 1 minute. Add the pork, prawns, salt and pepper, and stir-fry until heated through, about 2 to 3 minutes. Add a little more stock if needed. Add the spring onion and stir-fry for a few seconds.

6 Transfer to a large serving dish and serve with Sambal Belachan and limes on the side. Or, if preferred, small bowls of black soy sauce with sliced red chillies.

For variation, substitute fresh squid for half of the prawns. Slice cleaned squid into rings and simmer together with the prawns.

Vegetarian Beehoon

4 tablespoons oil

1 medium onion, halved and thinly sliced

5 dried black Chinese mushrooms, soaked in hot water to soften, stems discarded, caps thinly sliced

1 clove garlic, minced

1–2 red finger-length chillies, deseeded and thinly sliced

1 medium carrot, peeled and coarsely grated or sliced

1 medium green bell pepper, deseeded, cored and cut into thin strips

200 g (7 oz) *tau kwa* (pressed tofu), deep-fried until golden brown, then cut into strips

100 g (2 cups) bean sprouts, rinsed and cleaned

2 eggs, lightly beaten

1 tablespoon soy sauce

300 g (10 oz) dried *beehoon* (dried rice vermicelli), soaked in hot water to soften, then drained and cut into 10-cm (4-in) lengths

1 spring onion, cut into short lengths

Bottled or fresh chilli sauce or 1–2 red finger-length chillies, sliced

2–3 small green limes, quartered, to serve

1 Heat the oil in a wok over medium heat and stir-fry the onion until soft, about 2 minutes. Add the mushrooms, garlic and chillies, and stir-fry for 1 minute. Add the carrot and bell pepper, increase the heat to high and stir-fry for 2 minutes.

2 Add the *tau kwa* and bean sprouts, and stir-fry briskly for 30 seconds. Add the egg and allow it to set a little, about 15 seconds, then stir-fry briskly to mix well. Add the soy sauce and stir-fry to mix well.

3 Add the *beehoon* and spring onion, and stir-fry until heated through, about 1 minute. Transfer to a serving dish and serve with small sauce bowls of bottled or fresh chilli sauce or sliced chillies and lime on the side.

Serves 4–6
Preparation time: **20 mins**
Cooking time: **10 mins**

Murtabak (Indian Pancake with Meat Filling)

1 large egg, lightly beaten
1 large onion, finely diced

Dough
300 g (2 cups) plain flour
1 teaspoon salt
1 tablespoon ghee or butter
1 small egg, lightly beaten
125 ml ($^1/_2$ cup) milk
Warm water

125 ml ($^1/_2$ cup) oil

Filling
2 tablespoons oil
1 small onion, diced
1 clove garlic, minced
1 teaspoon finely grated
  fresh ginger
$^1/_2$ teaspoon turmeric
  powder

$^1/_2$ teaspoon chilli powder
350 g (12$^1/_2$ oz) minced
  lean lamb or beef
1 teaspoon *garam masala*
$^3/_4$–1 teaspoon salt

Serves 4–6
Preparation time: **30 mins**
  + standing time
Cooking time: **20 mins**

1 To make the Dough, sift the flour and salt into a large bowl then rub in the ghee. Put the egg and milk into a 250 ml cup and add warm water to make a 200 ml ($^3/_4$ cup) mixture. Make a well in the flour, and stir in egg mixture to make a soft dough. Transfer to an oiled board and knead until smooth and elastic, about 10 minutes. Add a little flour if the mixture seems sticky, or put all ingredients in a food processor fitted with a plastic blade and process at low speed for 3 minutes.

2 Divide the dough into 8 balls. Put the oil into a wide bowl. Add the balls, turning to coat with oil. Cover the bowl and leave in a warm place for 1 hour, or overnight.

3 To prepare the Filling, heat the oil in a wok and stir-fry the onion over medium heat until soft. Add the garlic and ginger and stir-fry 1 minute. Add the turmeric and chilli powder, stir a few seconds, then add the meat and stir-fry until it changes colour. Cover the wok and simmer for 15 minutes, adding a little water if the meat threatens to burn. Sprinkle with *garam masala* and salt, stir and cook uncovered for about 1 minute.

4 Place a dough ball on a greased surface. Press to stretch into a thin oval about 28 cm x 18 cm (11 x 7 in). Fold both sides towards the centre, pick up dough and squeeze gently to make a "rope" at least 30 cm (12 in) long. Coil the "rope" into a circle on a greased tray. Repeat with remaining dough balls, cover with plastic wrap, and leave for at least 30 minutes, or several hours.

5 Just before cooking, squeeze a coil of dough into a ball. Oil your hands and press out the dough with the palm of your hand to make a circle. Spread the dough out from the centre and gently pull the edges to stretch them as thinly as possible, to about 25 cm (10 in) in diameter.

6 Grease a large skillet with 1 tablespoon of the oil left in the bowl and heat. When the oil is very hot, put in dough. Smear with 1 tablespoon of the beaten egg, then scatter $^1/_8$ of the minced meat and $^1/_8$ of the chopped onion on top. Fold up like an envelope and cook until golden, 2 minutes. Turn and cook on the other side, adding a little more oil if the pan is too dry. Serve hot.

Classic Chicken Rice with Ginger Chilli Sauce

1 teaspoon rice wine
2 tablespoons soy sauce
1 very fresh chicken
(about 1$^1/_2$ kg/ 3 lbs)
2 slices fresh ginger
1 clove garlic, bruised
1 spring onion, chopped
1 teaspoon sesame oil
$^1/_2$ teaspoon salt
Coriander leaves
(cilantro), to garnish
Freshly sliced cucumber, to
garnish
Black soy sauce or regular
soy sauce, to serve

Rice
400 g (2 cups) uncooked
long-grain rice
1 litre (4 cups) Chicken
stock to cover rice by 2
cm ($^3/_4$ in)
$^1/_2$ tablespoon chicken
fat (optional)

Ginger Chilli Sauce
8–10 red finger-length
chillies, deseeded
2 cloves garlic, peeled
2 cm ($^3/_4$ in) fresh ginger,
peeled and sliced
2 teaspoons chicken
stock (from simmering
chicken)
$^1/_4$ teaspoon salt

Serves 4–6
Preparation time: 20 mins
Cooking time: 70 mins

1 Combine the rice wine and 2 teaspoons of the soy sauce, and rub this mixture inside the chicken. Place the ginger, garlic and spring onion inside the chicken.
2 Use a pot large enough to hold the chicken. Add enough water to cover the chicken and bring to a boil. Add the chicken, cover and turn off the heat. Allow the chicken to steep for 5 minutes. Then remove the chicken from the pot, drain the water from the stomach cavity and return the chicken to the pot. Cover and allow to steep for 25 minutes with the heat turned off.
3 Drain the chicken again and remove it from water. Bring the water back to a boil, remove from the heat, place the chicken back in the boiling water and steep the chicken for 30 minutes. By this time, it should be cooked; leave the chicken in the water until ready to serve.
4 To make the Ginger Chilli Sauce, grind all the ingredients in a mortar or blender until fine. Transfer to 4 small sauce bowls and set aside.
5 While the chicken is cooking, cook the Rice. Place the rice, chicken stock and chicken fat, if using, into a pan. Bring to a boil, then reduce the heat and simmer, covered, for 15 to 20 minutes until the rice is cooked. Alternatively, cook the rice in the stock in a rice cooker.
6 Combine the remaining soy sauce, sesame oil and salt in a small bowl. Drain the chicken and rub the soy mixture on the outside. Use a cleaver to slice the chicken, through the bones, into small serving slices. Place the chicken on a serving dish and garnish with coriander leaves and freshly sliced cucumber. Serve with small bowls of soy sauce and Ginger Chilli Sauce on the side.

To make a delicious chicken vegetable broth, reserve the chicken stock and skim the fat off. Bring to a boil, add sliced cabbage, carrot, salt and pepper to taste, and garnish with freshly sliced spring onions.

Diced Chicken with Dried Red Chillies

$^1/_2$ star anise pod or $^1/_2$ teaspoon ground star anise
10 black peppercorns or $^1/_2$ teaspoon freshly ground
  black pepper
1 teaspoon sugar
1 teaspoon soy sauce
1 teaspoon black Chinese vinegar
1 teaspoon rice wine
2 teaspoons cornflour
85 ml ($^1/_3$ cup) water
125 ml ($^1/_2$ cup) oil
500 g (1 lb) boneless chicken thigh or breast, cubed
1 teaspoon chopped crushed garlic
8–12 dried chillies, deseeded, sliced into short lengths
1 teaspoon finely grated or crushed ginger
2 spring onions, cut into short lengths
$^1/_4$ teaspoon sesame oil

1 Grind the star anise and peppercorns to a powder in a spice grinder. Set aside.
3 Mix the sugar, soy sauce, vinegar, rice wine, cornflour and water in a small bowl. Set aside.
4 Heat the oil in a wok over high heat until very hot and stir-fry the chicken until golden brown, about 2 minutes. Remove from the oil and drain on paper towels. Discard all but 1 tablespoon of the oil.
5 Heat the reserved oil in the wok over medium heat and stir-fry the chillies until they turn colour and begin to smoke, about 2–3 minutes. Immediately remove the chillies from the wok and set aside. Then add the ground spices, garlic and ginger to the wok and stir-fry 1 minute until fragrant. Add the sauce mixture and spring onions, and stir for 30 seconds, then return the chicken and chillies to the wok. Stir-fry 1 minute, drizzle with the sesame oil and serve immediately.

Serves 4
Preparation time: **10 mins**
Cooking time: **20 mins**

Gulai Ayam (Chicken in Spicy Coconut Milk)

2 tablespoons oil
1 chicken (about 1½ kg /3 lbs), cut into serving pieces
625 ml (2½ cups) coconut milk
2 stalks lemongrass, thick bottom third only, outer layers discarded, inner part bruised
1 teaspoon salt

Spice Paste
2 teaspoons cumin seeds
1 teaspoon fennel seeds
4 teaspoons coriander seeds
1 cinnamon stick (about 2 cm/¾ in)
4 candlenuts or macadamia nuts, chopped
6 shallots, peeled
3–4 dried chillies, cut into short lengths, soaked to soften, then deseeded
2 cloves garlic, minced
2 teaspoons freshly grated ginger
½ teaspoon ground turmeric
¼ teaspoon ground nutmeg

1 To make the Spice Paste, dry-fry the cumin, fennel, coriander and cinnamon over low heat in a skillet until fragrant, about 1 minute. Remove from the heat and allow to cool. Then grind the spices to a powder in a dry grinder or blender. Add the candlenuts or macadamia nuts, shallots, chillies, garlic and ginger, and grind to a paste, adding a little oil if necessary to keep the mixture turning. Add the ground turmeric and nutmeg, and mix well.

2 Heat the oil in a wok and add the Spice Paste. Stir-fry over low to medium heat, 4–5 minutes. Add the chicken pieces and stir-fry until they change colour and are coated with the Spice Paste, about 5 minutes.

3 Add the coconut milk, lemongrass and salt and bring slowly to a boil, stirring constantly. Simmer gently with the wok uncovered, stirring from time to time, until the chicken is cooked and the sauce has thickened, 30–35 minutes. Transfer to a bowl and serve hot with steamed rice.

Serves 4–6
Preparation time: 15 mins
Cooking time: 35 mins

Chicken Satay with Peanut Sauce

1 kg (2 lbs) chicken breast or thigh meat, sliced into bite-sized chunks
Bamboo skewers, soaked in water for several hours
1 stalk lemongrass, thick bottom third only, outer layers discarded, inner part bruised
Oil, for brushing
1 small cucumber, cut into chunks
1 large red onion, cut into wedges

Peanut Sauce
8 shallots
1 clove garlic
8 dried chillies, cut into lengths, deseeded, then soaked to soften
1 cm ($^1/_2$ in) fresh galangal root, peeled
1 stalk lemongrass, thick bottom third only, outer layers discarded
3 tablespoons oil
$^1/_2$ tablespoon tamarind pulp, mashed in 2 tablespoons warm water, strained to obtain juice
75 g ($^1/_2$ cup) raw peanuts, dry-roasted, or $^1/_2$ cup chunky peanut butter
250 ml (1 cup) thick coconut milk
1 tablespoon sugar
1 teaspoon salt

Marinade
1 tablespoon coriander
1 teaspoon cumin
$^1/_2$ teaspoon fennel
8 shallots, chopped
1 cm ($^1/_2$ in) fresh turmeric root or 1 teaspoon turmeric powder
1 cm ($^1/_2$ in) ginger
2 teaspoons sugar

Serves 6
Preparation time: **45 mins**
Cooking time: **15 mins +**
   35 mins grilling time

1 To prepare the Marinade, lightly dry-roast the coriander, cumin and fennel in a skillet, then process to a powder in a spice grinder. Add all remaining Marinade ingredients except for the tamarind juice and process to a smooth paste. Transfer to a large bowl and stir in tamarind juice, then add the chicken, stirring to mix well. Set aside while preparing the sauce.

2 To make the Peanut Sauce, process the chillies, shallots, garlic, galangal and lemongrass until finely ground. Heat the oil in a small pan and add the ground mixture, stir-frying over medium heat for 4–5 minutes. Add the tamarind juice, peanuts, salt and sugar. Bring to the boil, stirring, then lower heat and simmer until the sauce thickens. Transfer the sauce to a bowl and leave to cool.

3 Thread the chicken pieces onto soaked bamboo skewers. Brush with the lemongrass dipped in oil and cook over hot charcoal or under a broiler grill, turning until golden brown and cooked on both sides, brushing once or twice more with the oil. Place the satays on a serving plate, garnish with cucumber and onion wedges, and serve with small bowls of the Peanut Sauce.

Teochew Braised Soy Duck

1 fresh or frozen duck
(about 2$^1/_2$ kg/5 lbs)
2 teaspoons five spice
powder
$^1/_2$ teaspoon salt
60 ml ($^1/_4$ cup) black soy
sauce
2 tablespoons soy sauce
2 tablespoons sugar
750 ml (3 cups) water
4 cloves garlic, skin left
on, lightly bruised
1 cinnamon stick (about
3 cm/1$^1/_4$ in)
5 thin slices fresh galangal
or ginger

Dipping Sauce
4 tablespoons black
Chinese vinegar
1 tablespoon water
1 tablespoon finely
chopped garlic

1 Remove the fatty deposits from inside the duck and trim away any loose skin. Wash, drain and pat the duck dry with paper towels.

2 Combine the five spice powder, salt and both soy sauces. Rub the duck inside and out with this mixture then set aside to marinate for 2 hours, turning occasionally, rubbing and spooning the marinade over the duck.

3 Put the sugar in a wok with 2 tablespoons of the water and cook until it begins to caramelise and turn golden brown. Quickly add the remaining water, garlic, cinnamon and the marinade from the duck. Place the galangal or ginger slices inside the duck and put the duck into the wok. Bring to a boil, cover and simmer until the duck is tender, 1$^1/_2$–2 hours, turning the duck from time to time to ensure it cooks evenly.

4 While the duck is cooking, combine all Dipping Sauce ingredients and divide into 4 small dipping bowls.

5 When the duck is cooked, cut into serving portions and arrange on a large platter. Pour over some of the cooking liquid and serve with the Dipping Sauce.

Serves 4–6
Preparation time: 15 mins + 2 hours marinating
Cooking time: 2 hours

Gulai Kambing (Malay Lamb Stew)

12 shallots
3 cloves garlic
1 cm ($^1/_2$ in) fresh ginger
6 dried chillies, cut into
  lengths, deseeded, then
  soaked to soften
3 tablespoons oil
600 g (1$^1/_4$ lb) lean lamb
  meat, cut into cubes
375 ml (1$^1/_2$ cups) water
1 teaspoon salt
125 ml ($^1/_2$ cup) thick
  coconut milk
1 tablespoon tamarind
  juice (page 5)

Spice Paste
4 teaspoons coriander
2 teaspoons cumin
1 teaspoon fennel
2 cm ($^3/_4$ in) cinnamon
4 cloves
$^1/_4$ teaspoon black
  peppercorns
$^1/_8$ whole nutmeg
$^1/_4$ teaspoon turmeric
  powder
1$^1/_2$ tablespoons water

1 To prepare the Spice Paste, dry-roast the coriander, cumin, fennel, cinnamon, cloves, peppercorns and nutmeg in a skillet or small saucepan over low heat, shaking the pan frequently, until the spices become fragrant, about 2 minutes. Transfer to a spice grinder and process to a fine powder. Transfer to a bowl, add the turmeric and stir in the water to make a stiff paste.

2 Process the shallots, garlic, ginger and chillies in a spice grinder until fine, adding a little of the oil if necessary to keep the mixture turning. Heat the oil in a wok then stir-fry the shallot mixture over medium heat for about 4 minutes.

3 Add the Spice Paste and stir-fry for 3 minutes. Add lamb and stir-fry until it changes colour and is covered with spices, about 4 minutes. Add the water and salt, cover the wok and simmer until the meat is tender, about 45–60 minutes.

4 Add the coconut milk and tamarind juice and simmer gently, uncovered, until the sauce has thickened and the meat is very tender, about 15 minutes. Serve hot with white rice or crusty French bread.

Serves 4–6
Preparation time: **20 mins**
Cooking time: **1 hour 15 mins**

Tau Yu Bak (Pork Braised In Black Sauce)

600 g (1 1/4 lb) belly
  or shoulder pork, skin
  left on
3 tablespoons black soy
  sauce
3 tablespoons soy sauce
2 teaspoons sugar
1/4 teaspoon white
  pepper
10 shallots
4 cloves garlic
1 tablespoon oil
1 tablespoon *tau cheo*
  (salted soy beans—
  page 19)
8 dried black Chinese
  mushrooms, soaked
  to soften, stems
  discarded
1 litre (4 cups) water
150 g (5 oz) canned
  bamboo shoots, cut
  into wedges, or 2–3
  potatoes, peeled and
  quartered

1 Cut the pork into thick slices, then into bite-sized chunks. Sprinkle with both types of soy sauce, sugar and pepper. Mix well and leave to marinate for 30 minutes.

2 Process the shallots and garlic in a blender or grinder until finely ground. Heat the oil in a wok or large saucepan, then add the processed mixture and stir-fry over medium heat for 2 minutes. Add the *tau cheo* and stir-fry for 30 seconds. Add the mushrooms and stir-fry for 1 minute.

3 Remove the meat from the marinade, reserving the marinade. Add the meat to the wok and stir-fry until it changes colour, 3–4 minutes. Add the water and reserved marinade and bring to a boil. Reduce heat, cover and simmer until the meat is just tender, about 45 minutes.

4 Add the bamboo shoots or potatoes. Cover and simmer, stirring occasionally, until the meat is very soft and the sauce has thickened, 15–20 minutes. Serve hot with steamed white rice.

Serves 4–6
Preparation time: **15 mins + 30 mins marinating**
Cooking time: **1 hour 10 mins**

Chinese Beef Steak

675 g (1$^1/_2$ lbs) beef steak, sliced into bite-sized pieces
1 tablespoon cornflour
1 teaspoon baking soda
1 tablespoon soy sauce
1 tablespoon steak sauce
1 teaspoon rice wine
$^1/_2$ teaspoon sesame oil
1 egg
4 tablespoons oil
1 teaspoon finely minced garlic
Steamed asparagus or broccoli, to serve

Sauce
185 ml ($^3/_4$ cup) water
1 tablespoon Worcestershire sauce
1 tablespoon tomato ketchup
1 teaspoon oyster sauce
1 teaspoon sugar
$^1/_2$ teaspoon salt

Serves 4
Preparation time: **15 mins + 4–8 hours marinating**
Cooking time: **10 mins**

1 Place the meat in a bowl, sprinkle with the corn-flour, then sift the baking soda into the bowl and stir with a wooden spoon to coat the meat well. Add the soy sauce, steak sauce, rice wine, sesame oil, egg and 2 tablespoons of the oil, then mix well. Refrigerate the meat in a covered container, stirring occasionally, for 4–8 hours.
2 Combine the Sauce ingredients in a small bowl, stir-ring to dissolve the sugar and salt, then set aside.
3 When ready to cook, drain the meat and discard the marinade.
4 Heat the remaining oil in a wok, add the garlic and cook until golden brown. Increase the heat, add the meat and stir-fry until the meat changes colour, about 3 minutes. Add the Sauce, cover the wok, and simmer gently until the meat is well cooked and the gravy reduced to a thick sauce, 3–5 minutes.
5 Place the meat and sauce on a serving plate with the steamed asparagus or broccoli and serve immediately.

Oyster sauce is the rich, thick and dark extract of dried oysters. It is frequently added to stir-fried vegetable and meat dishes, and must be refrigerated once the bottle is opened. Expensive versions made with abalone and vegetarian versions made from mushrooms are also available. Check the ingredients listed on the bottle as many brands are loaded with MSG.

Soy Braised Pork Leg

1 pork leg (preferably front leg), about 1 kg (2 lbs)
125 ml (¹/₂ cup) oil
125 g (4 oz) *tau fu kee* (dried twisted tofu skin), wiped
  with a damp cloth, cut into 5-cm (2-in) lengths
3–4 cloves garlic, smashed and minced
1 tablespoon *tau cheo* (salted soy beans—page 19)
2 thin slices fresh ginger
4 dried black Chinese mushrooms, soaked to soften,
  stems discarded, soaking liquid reserved
1¹/₂ teaspoons *nam yee* (fermented red tofu), mashed
  with a fork
2 tablespoons soy sauce
2 tablespoons black soy sauce
Water for cooking pork

1 Wipe the pork leg with a damp cloth to clean, then
set aside. Heat the oil in a wok and fry the *tau fu kee*
pieces, a few at a time, until they puff up and turn
golden. Drain on paper towels.
2 Pour out all but 1 tablespoon of the oil from the wok.
Stir-fry the garlic over medium heat until golden.
Add the *tau cheo* and stir-fry 1 minute, then add the
pork leg, ginger, mushrooms and *nam yee*. Stir-fry
for 5 minutes.
3 Transfer all ingredients to a pot that is just big enough
to hold the pork leg. Add both types of soy sauce, the
mushroom soaking liquid and enough water to just
cover the pork. Bring to a boil, cover, and simmer until
the pork is very tender, turning the leg a couple of times
so that it cooks evenly, about 40–50 minutes. Serve
hot with steamed rice.

Nam yee or fermented red tofu is preserved in wine,
salt and spices and sold in jars. It keeps almost
indefinitely on the shelf but should be refrigerated
once opened.

Serves 4
Preparation time: **10 mins**
Cooking time: **50 mins**

Crispy Barbequed Pork Ribs

1 1/2 litres (6 cups) water
900 g (2 lbs) meaty pork
  ribs, cut into serving
  portions
1 1/2 tablespoons honey
1 tablespoon soy sauce
1 tablespoon black soy
  sauce
1 tablespoon rice wine
1 tablespoon black
  Chinese vinegar
1 tablespoon sugar
1 teaspoon five spice
  powder
1 teaspoon salt
1 teaspoon sesame oil
500 ml (2 cups) chicken
  stock (made fresh or
  from stock cubes)
1 teaspoon toasted
  sesame seeds, to gar-
  nish
1 medium carrot, grated,
  to garnish
Lettuce leaves, to serve
Bottled sweet chilli sauce,
  to serve

1 Bring the water to a boil in the pot. Blanch the ribs for 5 minutes, then drain, discarding the water.

2 Place the ribs in a bowl and sprinkle them with the honey, light and black soy sauces, rice wine, vinegar, sugar, five spice powder, salt and sesame oil. Stir carefully with a wooden spoon to mix thoroughly and set aside to marinate for 30 minutes.

3 When ready to cook, transfer the ribs and the marinade to a wok or wide saucepan and add the chicken stock. Bring to a boil, cover and simmer for 15 minutes, stirring several times. Transfer the ribs to a bowl. Bring the cooking liquid back to a boil and cook over very high heat, uncovered, until the mixture reduces and becomes thick and syrupy, about 15 minutes.

4 Pour the mixture over the pork ribs and stir with a wooden spoon for about 1 minute to coat the ribs thoroughly with the mixture. Drain the ribs in a colander.

5 Preheat an oven broiler, then arrange the ribs on a rack set into an oven tray and grill under high heat for 8–10 minutes on each side.

6 Sprinkle with sesame seeds and serve the ribs hot on a bed of lettuce and grated carrots with chilli sauce on the side.

Serves 4
Preparation time: **10 mins + 30 mins marinating**
Cooking time: **2 hours**

Sweet Mung Bean Soup

150 g ($^1/_2$ cup) split green (mung) beans, rinsed, washed
  and soaked in 1 litre (4 cups) water for 30 minutes
1 litre (4 cups) water
4 fresh pandanus leaves, tied in a knot, or $^1/_4$ teaspoon
  pandanus essence
5 tablespoons sugar
4 tablespoons water chestnut flour, mixed with
  60 ml ($^1/_4$ cup) water, or 3 tablespoons arrowroot
  flour mixed with 3 tablespoons water
4–6 *yu tiao* (fried Chinese crullers), cut into
  bite-sized pieces

1 Drain the beans and place them in a steaming basket
lined with a piece of muslin cloth. Steam over boiling
water for 30–40 minutes until soft.
2 Place the water, pandanus leaves or essence, and sugar
in a large pot. Stir for 5 minutes over medium heat
until the sugar completely dissolves. Bring to a boil.
3 Stir the water chestnut or arrowroot mixture to mix
well. Slowly drizzle the mixture into the boiling liquid,
stirring continuously, until the liquid thickens to
desired consistency.
4 Remove the steamed beans from the steaming basket
and add them to the pot containing the starchy liquid.
5 Return to a boil. Remove from the heat, discard the
pandanus leaves if using. Serve hot, garnished with
pieces of *yu tiao* (fried Chinese crullers).

Serves 4–6
Preparation time: **40 mins**
Cooking time: **30 mins**

Goreng Pisang (Deep-fried Bananas)

125 g (1 cup) plain flour
80 g (¹/₂ cup) rice flour
2 teaspoons baking
  powder
¹/₄ teaspoon salt
250 ml (1 cup) water
Oil, for deep-frying
4 large or 8 small firm
  ripe bananas, peeled
  (and cut into sections if
  using large bananas)

1 Sift both types of flour with the baking powder and salt into a bowl. Gradually stir in the water to make a thick batter.

2 Heat the oil in a wok. Dip the bananas into the batter, turning to coat thoroughly. When the oil is very hot, add the bananas and deep-fry until golden brown, about 4 minutes. Drain thoroughly and serve warm.

Serves 4
Preparation time: **10 mins**
Cooking time: **10 mins**

Sweet White Fungus and Lotus Seeds

20 g (¹/₂ oz) dried white fungus
70 g (2¹/₂ oz) dried shelled lotus seeds
125 g (8 oz) rock sugar
2 tablespoons white sugar, or more to taste
1 litre (4 cups) water
Crushed ice or ice cubes
1 can longans, drained (optional)

Serves 4–6
Preparation time: **25 mins**
Cooking time: **45 mins**

1 Place the fungus in a bowl and add hot water to cover. Soak for 15 minutes, then cut away any hard or discoloured portions and cut the rest into bite-sized pieces.

2 Split open the lotus seeds and flick out the dark bitter cores with the point of a knife.

3 Put the soaked fungus, lotus seeds, rock sugar and white sugar in a saucepan with the water. Cover and simmer gently until the lotus seeds and fungus are soft, about 1 hour. Add more sugar if desired, depending on how much ice you will use later. Transfer to a bowl and when cool, refrigerate until required.

4 To serve, spoon the syrup, fungus and lotus seeds into 4 soup bowls. Add ice and canned longans, if desired, then serve with soup spoons.

Index